NEVER BEEN SINGLE

A JOURNEY OF SELF-WORTH

PRIYANNSHA

NU VOICE PRESS

First published by NU VOICE PRESS 2025
An imprint of Hubhawks Pvt. Ltd
www.nuvoicepress.com

ISBN: 978-81-992047-5-1

Printedat Thomson Press (India) Ltd.

Published by: Nu Voice Press

For my Father,

Whose unconditional love lets me be whoever I want to be.

& To all the people who dream big, even when they are told not to.

Table of Contents

The One Who Chooses Family Over Love

So, we all think we should applaud people who do that, people who choose family over love. But in all honesty, it's a difficult choice, to live the life of a Martyr or a rebel in the other case. I frankly have no idea about the Martyr side, because I have always done as I bloody well wished for. What's unfathomable to me is how someone can leave one love for another. I think they are trained, very well trained to do so by their so-called practical families. I have been called an emotional fool by many such people. Maybe I am, and I have made many more mistakes than these people. I just don't want any regrets later in life. I don't want to be lying on my deathbed, and thinking what if?

Breaking news! You can love your family to the moon and back and still do what you damn well please with your life. Unless of course, you are co-dependently existing with yours, emotionally, I mean. At this point, I must ask, "What kind of family would like you to give up on love and for what?" Well, there can be many types across the world. No, it's not only the Indian families.

However, I wish you wouldn't be this person; I have seen many of them up close. They just keep trying too hard in every area of their life but are mostly unhappy. I presume choosing one over another can be a soul-breaking experience.

Trust me, I am not judging, but only wondering. Has it ever occurred to them that they will die? I mean, we all will. We also forget this important truth all the time. I wonder what kind of practical bullshit they tell themselves to leave the one they love, or maybe, it's not love after all.

I have immense gratitude to God for giving me a family that thrives on love. I was left by someone I truly loved because that person thought I wasn't right for their family. It was unbearably painful. It did break my heart, but not my soul. The soul has always been intact. Heartbreaks are painful just like if you break any of your limbs, but it mends; sometimes it might take longer. Suppressing the soul is a whole different story altogether. When you suppress the calling of your soul for a person, a thing or a vocation, it creates a huge tear inside, and nothing can fill that. I wish more power to the Martyrs, and hope they did it for the right reasons.

I would rather be a rebel any day and be with someone who considers me family, so that he doesn't have to choose now, does he? Also, my lovelies, however much your heart pains, always remember: Rejections are Divine Protection. I believe in this as strongly as I believe in love. Be with someone who chooses you always, come what may. And for God's sake, don't be emotionally dependent on your family for happiness.

Affirmation: I can choose myself over my Family when needed.

BE THERE FOR OTHERS, BUT NEVER LEAVE YOURSELF BEHIND – DODINSKY

Self-Worth and Receiving Help

Since we were little children, we have always looked up to Strong people as our aspirational models. We wish to be strong; the stronger, the better. No one has taught us to be vulnerable, and of course, everyone has forgotten to mention, that vulnerability at the right time can also be a superpower.

There will be times in your life when people will come and help you. It will be when you need it the most. At that time, if your self-worth blocks it or you view taking help as a weakness, life gets much harder. I have seen the strongest of people needing help at one or the other time in their lives. These periods of vulnerability in our lives make us human; and make us who we are. When you are about to lose your shit, if a helping hand comes, take it. Accepting help when you need it is also a sign of strength. You do not have to do it all alone.

Well, why go far, as I am a classic example of this block. I would just give and give, but it made me miserable after a point. Why would I not get help? It affected my self-worth. Even if I did take it, I would immediately give the same amount or more back to that person. Not only did I suffer due to this, but all my relationships started suffering too. There was a constant internal battle that I had to fight.

So now I have no issues in receiving. I still give a lot. I have a problem there. Good thing, though I have started to receive and ask. There is no shame in asking, as they say the baby who cries gets the milk. Ask and you shall receive, even the heavens need you to ask. When I take or receive help, I realise I deserve it and hence, it is coming to me. Why should we take it? Well, why not? It does not make you any less strong; it just makes you more relatable. Also, sometimes people around you will wish to help you, don't take this feeling away from them.

Just make sure your self-worth remains unaffected and ask away. We all need help; we cannot do it alone, however great or talented we are. So put your ego on the side and receive it.

Affirmation: I can easily receive help. I ask for help when needed. My self-worth remains unaffected when I receive help.

NO TEAM WORKS OUT TEAMWORK – DWYANE WADE

Self-Worth and Someone Else Loving You

As I write this chapter, I feel I have arrived here too late, in life, I mean. I wish I had known this before, but I am glad that at least you are reading this now. I have always handed over my sense of self and self-worth to people who loved me. It is a horrendous idea, of course, but I didn't know any better. But why on earth would I do that? I wasn't doing it consciously. It just happens when you are unhealed, and your inner child has been devoid of that unconditional love from at least one person. Every child needs at least that one person who loves them unconditionally, which is why I am that person for the kids in my family now. I know better now. When your inner child seeks love, your self-worth automatically becomes dependent on whoever loves you. It constantly keeps travelling from your Mother to your Father to your Brother, to your Partner, maybe to your Best friend. It is never with you.

"Children need at least one person in their life who thinks that the sun rises and sets on them, someone who takes delight in their existence and loves them unconditionally."

So, if you were that child who grew up without the approval and unconditional love of many people, or at least one person, you will be like me mostly. Brave and Strong, but unaware that we are not anchored in our sense of self, but rather, in whoever is showering love at that moment. At this point, you might retort that you have a high level of self-love, but it will not work unless someone else is also loving you and approving of you in every way. Let's say your relationship status with you is complicated. It is like having a light inside, but the switch is in someone else's hand. Super weird, right? You will be surprised how many people have this issue.

Your switch to shine should be in your hand, not anyone else's. I am writing this chapter close to Diwali, thus the reference to lights. What I am essentially getting at is that you should not wait to shine till someone comes along and decides to fall in love with you. At any point in your life, if you feel that no one loves you the way you wish to be loved, remember that you are not alone. You love yourself, invest in yourself, clap for yourself, and be kind and generous to yourself. It is easier than you think it is. Do not, I repeat, do not cling to toxic relationships just because there must be someone to cheer you on. I feel those relationships will dim your shine anyway. I am sure no one has told you this; sometimes seclusion can bring you closer to yourself, and more often than not, it leads to greatness. Of course, I am not asking you to be in permanent seclusion, but if a time arises like this, don't be afraid. Why are we so afraid of being alone anyway? When you are alone, you must face yourself in your complete truth, and it will bring out your true self.

It brings about a lot of change and metamorphosis. If you wish to live your authentic best life, don't be so afraid to be alone. You will need those times also in your life.

My whole point with this chapter is that if you are waiting to find the treasure you are holding within, to reveal your true greatness only when your earth-shattering love arrives, stop waiting. Do it on your own. For this, you will have to heal that inner child and love yourself a lot more. It will bring about a lot of emotions, deal with them, cry, howl, break things, and do whatever it takes. Because after that you will fly!

Affirmations: My self-love and worth are unaffected by external love.

My self-worth is fuelled by my self-love.

I can shine on my own.

IT IS DURING OUR DARKEST MOMENTS THAT WE MUST FOCUS TO SEE THE LIGHT – ARISTOTLE

Self-Worth and How You Treat Yourself in the Face of Adversity, Aka, Tough Times

(When things that you don't expect to happen to you, happen)

The second most feared card in the tarot deck, after death (which actually means transformation), is the TOWER. It means a sudden, unexpected change. It is a rather scary card to look at; a tower is falling down, and two people are flying off this tower downwards. When it comes to your reading, something will change rather suddenly.

What if your life pulls out a tower on you? One fine day, everything you have built suddenly washes down and breaks down. Of course, it happens to all of us at some point, to a greater or lesser degree. We are also affected by it to varying degrees, depending on our ability to face adversity. Relationships fail, businesses fail, you get sick and/or you lose a loved one. Anything can happen at any time. We are affected materially by any material catastrophe, but sometimes, the cycle gets really long. You are going through a long cycle of things not working out for you, which is when we say you are going through tough times. It does affect us emotionally, physically, financially and in my case, even hormonally. I believe the greatest impact it has is on our self-worth. It renders us devoid of hope and makes us fearful. We get distrustful about times changing and things getting better. We lose our self-belief that we can actually achieve things. Like, if you have been single for a very long time and all you have had are bad experiences, you stop believing in love. But the worst part is we stop believing in our capabilities and worth because of this so-called cycle of things happening to us one after another or over a long period of time. It totally gets to us in the wrong way. As Jen-Luc Picard said, "It's possible to commit no mistakes and still lose. That is not a weakness; that is life."

How do we cope with it? Well, it is going to be really shitty. You must accept that. Most people will run away, some quickly, some after a while, but in hindsight, you will find that a long period of struggle is a great gift indeed. Because when you have nothing to lose, you can go after anything. You can really explore your options, your capabilities and abilities at this point, and you will lose all fear due to the continuous struggle. All your so-called social connections will run away, barring a few true people. There is no one to influence you, and your true light can shine in this dark time. More often than not, you are going to become a badass in this scenario.

So, appreciate yourself if you have gone through this adversity, this period of catastrophic change or tumultuous transformation. Others might not understand it. When you take a moment to understand what is happening and just accept it's just the times and it has no bearing on you as such, your self-worth will return, and then you will light up in your full glory. Because now you already are a badass, remember? Do not stop believing in yourself if life throws some curveballs at you. You only need one good ball to strike. Rest if you must, but do not give up, as the wheel of fortune keeps turning always. Keep hustling, as there is always something you can do, as per my experience, however, the times are.

Affirmation:"I can face any adversity with my self-worth intact.

"Every adversity I face makes me stronger."

ONCE YOU CHOOSE HOPE, ANYTHING IS POSSIBLE – CHRISTOPHER REEVE

The One Who is Never Sure

Feeling safe and secure in a relationship is really important for me; it is one of my first conditions, and a person who is not sure will not be sure, even if they marry you. How do I know? I married someone I wasn't sure about, and that feeling never went away. And in hindsight, I was never sure because that person was entirely wrong for me. So, I worked on myself; I first figured out what I wanted from my life and relationships to be able to decide and be sure about someone. Because someone who has not done that work will possibly not be sure, not even about themselves, so don't expect them to be sure about you. If you are confused, you will attract confusing energy. See, living with someone who is not sure about you or thinks they have made a mistake is plain hurtful, and I do not recommend doing that.

Do enjoy what pops up in your life at that moment, even if it is engaging in a song war with one of your neighbours. Who knows, that may be what you need at that time. Do not fall in love with someone, I repeat, do not fall in love with someone who is not sure about you. I always say don't choose regret, choose to jump, but don't jump in a whirlpool of confusion. Have patience till you are assured and till the other person gives you signs of utmost certainty. We all know love is great, till it is not.

Affirmation: I Choose Clarity over Confusion.

THERE IS NO HARM IN REPEATING A GOOD THING – PLATO

The One Who is Running after His Dreams

It will be a rather short one, this story. When someone is running after their dreams, don't intercept them. By the way, what are you doing waiting for them? You should be running after your dreams, too. Now, whether it is a sprint or a marathon, or you meet someone at the start line, in the middle or at the finish line, it's all good. But you do not stop when you meet someone, you keep running. Do not sit and wait around for someone. You maintain your focus like before. Sounds Brutal, right? You know what is brutal is when you give up on your dreams and you get neither. The future with anyone is not certain, so at least do what you can for certainty, pick your dreams. And life can surprise you, as you might get both, but at least you are getting one. Thank me later.

Allow the other also to chase their dreams. If this person has stumbled upon you, they can't be expected to leave everything else in your pursuit. The same rules apply to both. Both of you should propel each other towards your dreams and not impede. The first step is to choose and follow yours.

P.S. If you are one of their dreams, they will pursue you in a healthy manner.

Affirmation: I choose my dreams every time.

THE SINGLE MOST POWERFUL THING I CAN BE IS TO BE MYSELF – DWAYNE JOHNSON

The Black Hole

When you are love, are light, are happy, and have worked on yourself enough, everyone will want to be with you. Be careful of the 'Black holes' at that time. These are generally good human beings with a lot of baggage and hurt in their heart. They are here to take from you. They will put all their burdens on you, emotional, spiritual, financial and even physical. They will suck the light out of you.

What if you start loving them? (Well, it can happen to anyone.) It will be a very difficult choice. You will have to choose between your love for them and your love for yourself. It will be an insane amount of work to be with such a person, and I have seen people get exhausted in about six months or a year. I have never seen a successful case of someone filling up that person with love and making them happy, because it is impossible to do it unless they work towards it. Now, people who are in love with them constantly tell me that they are changing, and they are now not the same. But my advice to those people and to you is to pick yourself. It is not about being selfish in love, as love is selfless, right? But does it have to be that sacrificial, really, and should the other person also not contribute and participate in this process? I am not talking about temporary phases of sorrow, but talking about a person who is unwilling to work on their sorrow and pain. I have seen my friends who have been in such relationships getting miserable by the day. If you love them, get them help, don't sacrifice yourself at their altar. The point is that healing, counselling or anything for that matter will work only if they are willing to work, and if you are doing everything for them, they just won't work on themselves. It is a vicious cycle, and you very well know why you get stuck in it. When you bloody can't love yourself, so even if a black hole comes along, you will readily get sucked in. God forbid that you have to love yourself; then you will not make choices that will get you to such places and people.

Now, sometimes people marry them. I am not a judgmental person. You can howl and cry that you genuinely love them, or you love each other. It's your free will, but if you step into that black hole, you can say goodbye to your dreams. It's bye-bye to you at all levels. My two cents are—don't. Wait till you collide with a star. Save your light for yourself till then, and for God's effing sake, love yourself enough till then.

Affirmation: I choose to save my light for myself.

ONLY IN THE DARKNESS CAN YOU SEE THE STARS
– MARTIN LUTHER KING JR.

Dilwale Dulhania Le Jayenge (The Cinderella Syndrome)

This nonsense we have been fed all this while, and the way we have lapped it up, like a thirsty puppy on a hot day. Well, who doesn't want to be rescued by a loaded, charming guy/girl, but what happens after that? When they take their so-called bride/groom/princess/ prince, where are they taking them? Their kingdom, is it? What is the taking of one's job? It's never specified except that there is only a dream of love and practically no other ambition. It is like being in a foreign country on a dependent visa. Trust me, it sucks, quite literally.

So even if you manifest the man of your dreams (please change for other genders) Not even once does he ask you about your hopes, dreams and ambitions, and worse is that when he does, he doesn't give two shits about it. What if she wants to become something or do something else? Will he come along? Or change his lifestyle? Well, ***Dulhania le to jayenge*** but ***kya sambhal payenge***? (They can rescue the princess, but can they keep the princess?) Have they tallied their dreams, goals and life? Values? What if the Prince wants only material success and the princess wants inner peace or vice versa? What will happen then? Can you stay in a gilded cage of love when you don't have inner happiness? I choose peace over love any day, will you? I suppose it is a different answer for everyone, as it should be.

So, all this romantic bullshit of someone coming and rescuing you or taking you to your dreamland; stop buying and selling it. I am not a killer of romance. Romance is in the small and big things others do for you. But I don't endorse this extreme notion of someone else coming and transforming your life, as it is impractical. Firstly, get out of the victim zone—you don't need rescuing. Everyone has problems gal. Resolve and fix your issues on your own. You can do it, irrespective of what they are. Secondly, have a life you love. Why do you even want to be scooped out of your own life and go to an alien land? It's so uncomfortable. Plant your own garden and bring flowers to your own self. Then when you meet someone, make mutual decisions of settling or uprooting, as you feel is right. As Alice Little said, "As traumatised children, we always dreamed that someone would come and save us. We never dreamed that it would be ourselves, as adults."

Let it come to you. First peace, then love. Always remember this sequence, as love cannot withstand the lack of peace for very long. And if it remains without peace, then it is not love but something else; mostly fear of being alone, among other things.

Affirmation: I let go of the need for someone else to rescue me and start to fix my own issues myself.

AVOID POPULARITY IF YOU WOULD HAVE PEACE
– ABRAHAM LINCOLN

Self-Worth and Rejection

Sometimes in life, when someone you deeply love rejects you, you seek acceptance from others to heal that wound. It can be a parent or a partner—someone you love unconditionally. Most of the time, when you are looking for acceptance, it results in a series of rejections till you are left reeling in pain. Then you realise that the only person who can accept or reject you is you. Accept yourself totally and completely, and let go of this need to be accepted by another.

Affirmation: I accept myself totally and completely.

The only acceptance I need is my own acceptance.

WE CANNOT DIRECT THE WIND, BUT WE CAN ADJUST THE SAILS – ANONYMOUS

The One Who Wants You To Chase Him

There is nothing wrong with chasing someone you love. Is that true? I agree, a little bit of initial work is required. If it's a long duration of chasing, it is not healthy. Why would a person who likes you back, make you chase him/her? So, you lose your power in the relationship, and you will. When you chase someone, you feel powerless and helpless. You are dependent on their behaviour and gestures of rejection or acceptance. You are no longer standing in your power, and will for sure be suppressed in the relationship, even if it works out in the end. Also, it takes a lot of energy to chase someone so you can bid your Vision boards and wish lists goodbye. We all have a limited amount of energy as human beings, so use it wisely. As Albus Dumbledore told Harry Potter, "You are not known by your abilities, but by your choices."

When I said this to some of my friends, they literally became my enemies. Well, if I see you chasing someone that desperately, I only have kindness and compassion for you. I totally understand that it takes every ounce of strength not to choose this, not to chase the one who probably also likes you back. It is tough to choose your dreams because dreams are far away, and this person is right in front of you. Going after your dreams is scary, and this is safe. I know this, my friend. I have made some wrong choices, and I know that this is a difficult choice. But as I keep telling everyone around me, it took me 9 years, not 9 months, to give birth to this powerful human being that I am now, so I cannot lose it. There is nothing I would despise more than chasing someone. So, if someone makes me chase them, I will end up disliking them. I just can't, however great they are.

Now, when such a choice presents itself to you and when you meet an almost perfect fit for you, you have to choose whether to chase them or your dreams. Choose your dreams. Keep your power, and you will find another. Fulfil your dreams, and the world will chase you. Gather your courage and make the tough choice. I have seen many give in at this point. Why do you even have to choose? Why do you have to chase? You deserve better. You deserve a love that takes you closer to your dreams, not farther. Remember to take deep breaths and tell yourself you deserve better. You can have love and support and fulfilled dreams all at once. STOP THE CHASE.

Affirmation: I refuse to chase anyone anymore.

DEFINITENESS OF PURPOSE IS THE STARTING POINT OF ALL ACHIEVEMENT – W. CLEMENT STONE

Self-Belief

Without self-belief, you cannot make the right decisions and more importantly, you cannot let go of things which are not right for you. You would only chase a person when you have lost your self-belief. You certainly don't believe you can do better, so you chase after the best possible opportunity or person who comes along. It is quite irrational, and fear is the basis of this. Maybe you had a slew of negative experiences and rejections, or are influenced by the nonsense of age and body clock that has put you in this position. You do not genuinely think that you cannot have someone whom you would not have to chase. Believe in yourself, and wait for the one who likes you enough and gives you the attention you deserve. It goes for both genders. Heal whatever has affected this belief instead of chasing an ASSHAT. If you do not believe in yourself, WHO WILL?

Affirmation: I choose to believe in myself against all odds.

WHEN YOU THINK POSITIVE, GOOD THINGS HAPPEN – MATT KEMP

Standing In Your Power

The main issue here is not that we are not powerful, but that we are told to be less powerful to be liked more. Smile more. Why don't you smile more? You look nicer when you smile. I also look great when I smack jackasses. Why can't I do that more? Be more likeable and less powerful. Is this true? Well, unfortunately, it is. You will end up being more likable, but less power means less liking yourself.

Don't say that! Don't do this! Keep this hush-hush. Don't ask questions about money or anything important! Plus of course, there is a general public opinion about how one should behave. Like once a neighbour gave me unsolicited advice, of course, that I would have to compromise a lot after I got married, and I am too strong for it. So, she was implying I am not marriage material. I, in the first place, didn't ask her to evaluate my marriage materialness, but she thought it was her duty to tell me to be less powerful. Be less powerful. Don't fight. Don't stand up for yourself. Don't call the wrong things out. Look the other way when you are being wronged. Ignore the insults directed at your self-esteem! Be miserable, but Likeable. Revel in toxic relationships.

Well, I say, why don't you stand in your power and see what happens to you and the people around you? Oh, you think they won't like you. I have news for you, most people already don't like other people, as they have their own complex, weird reasons for it. And people who like you will like you anyway. So, stand, be powerful and speak your truth. Trust me, nothing will happen to you. Yes, you might shock some people for a while, or they might dislike you by a degree or two more. Who cares? The only side effect of this in the long run is that you will be really happy.

So, Get out of the victim zone. Become powerful financially, emotionally and physically. Yes, work out too, I mean. Then make your decisions rather than remake them. Look at your life, and review it. What would you like to do with it? The only person who is stopping you is you and the rotten beliefs you have been fed. If you are able to do it, you will SHINE, like a happy and bright human should.

Still confused about what this whole power business is? It just means that you make your own life decisions and do what makes you happy. And you can do it along with your duties. I am not asking you to forego them. You will face resistance, but just don't give in. It means putting to living your life like others want; be it your parents or your partner. It also does not mean you do not love them; it means you love yourself too. Don't take shit from anyone and call the nonsense out. This is a prerequisite. Value and respect wouldn't automatically fall in your lap. You will have to do it for yourself.

Why should you do it? For the sheer joy and wonder of it. It has been the single most life-changing experience of my life.

P.S. Again, being powerful does not mean standing alone or becoming super aggressive or picking fights just to make a point. Please be gentle with yourself and others while they absorb it. Also, remember, you may still make mistakes, but they will be your own mistakes. Even that will feel great.

Affirmation: I choose to stand in my power in every way possible.

WHY NOT GO OUT ON A LIMB? THAT'S WHERE THE FRUIT IS – MARK TWAIN

The Emotional Cheater

This one is usually really smart and difficult to catch. I feel emotional cheating is the worst, not that the other kind is good. Usually, this kind of cheater is cold-hearted and emotional at the same time, which is a lethal combination, and not good for you.

This person is only taking emotional advantage of you, and you have been unaware of it for the longest time. You are probably friend-zoned, but it does not feel like a friendship. Taking any kind of advantage is unfair, even if it's emotional. He/she is usually quite hurt and emotional himself, so you will wish to help them. You're rescuing another person because you are kind, but this person will drop you in a wink when you are not needed. It is very tough to evade this one. But you cannot let him do that, as he is not the one. Secondly, he is taking advantage of you. It might not only be emotional after a while, but it can also be financial (dirty minds, you). Hehe, it can be physical too. This one brings you a very important lesson—not to become emotionally dependent or attached to someone unless you are sure of their intent.

We melt too soon when someone comes to us hurting and in need. We wish to help, but we should not unless we know the whole story, which in this case, you will not know. This person will not open up emotionally, and even if they do, they will skip the important parts.

Long ago, a wise lady told me not to get into a relationship with a person who puts the entire blame on the partner. This one will. It's a tell-tale sign of an emotional cheater. He does not—remember this—have the capacity to be in a relationship when things get tough or to resolve things. He will not accept his contribution to the problem, and he does not love you, my darling. He only wants a shoulder and more, maybe. Do you want to be someone's shoulder, or do you want to be someone's heart? The choice is entirely yours.

Affirmations:

I have emotional freedom. I stand in my own emotional power.

I let go of anyone who wishes to take advantage of me and who does not serve my highest good.

TO BE THE BEST, YOU MUST BE ABLE TO HANDLE THE WORST – WILSON KANADI

Self-Worth and Success Types

There are all kinds of successful people in the world. I have observed that people immediately tend to compare themselves to a person they think is more successful than they are, and are also ready to change the course of their life as per that person. Just because someone else is doing something and is successful at it, it's not necessarily a good idea for you. If you follow someone else, it will not get you success, but only a shit load of unhappiness.

Success is made of many things in life, like Relationships, money, friendships, good looks, family, and the freedom to do what you like, time to enjoy your money and good health. The most important secret ingredient in this mix is: Inner joy. Inner joy is inversely proportional to comparison. You may have 8 out of 10 things you want, but when you meet someone who has that 9th and 10th only, those will suddenly become more important than the other 8 you have. It will make you deeply unhappy, and you will stop enjoying whatever you have. There goes your inner joy, bye-bye!

I do not know what your success mix is. It is your job to find that out. Maybe it has 8 things or 3. Maybe 5. It is totally up to you. We all are different and have different capabilities, different gifts, and different life purposes. We cannot, and should not, adhere to one criterion of success.

For someone, relationships can be more important than a job. For some people, doing what they love can be the most important thing. For me, finding my calling was the most important; it made me deeply unhappy not to know what I was supposed to do with my life, despite having everything material that I needed. It is so unique to everyone that even if you do achieve someone else's success type, it gives you no joy or a very short-lived joy.

Like everything given by Mother Nature has a purpose, so do you. Find it. Find what makes you happy and be okay with it, whatever it is, even if it's vastly different from what you had imagined it to be. Do whatever makes you revel in 'inner joy,' because we are here to be joyful, and not here to pit ourselves against each other.

Affirmations: I define my own success. I follow my own true purpose, and it fills me with inner joy.

I let go of any comparison with anyone else and focus on my own goals and dreams.

HAPPINESS IS NOT SOMETHING READY-MADE. IT COMES FROM YOUR OWN ACTIONS – THE DALAI LAMA

Self-Worth Associated with Family Approval and Acknowledgement

Family love is the strongest, but it yields power over you. More often than not, we look to our family for approval, even for small decisions in our life. If not family, we will have friends who we consider family. Their approval and acknowledgement really matter to us. Sometimes, though, things can happen in your life which can put your family and friends out of depth. They might not have the emotional or intellectual capacity to deal with that situation or the life event. At that time, if your self-worth is deeply associated with their approval or acknowledgement, you won't be able to sail through it as you should have. Like, in more than one case I have seen people stay in abusive or unfulfilling relationships because they do not want to lose their family's approval or family's love.

It is no easy feat to do it all alone, so no judgment. It only makes your life restricted to your family's horizon. They can only grow to a point, that their family's collective mind allows. The moment they try to step out, they are gripped with fear, which is natural for everyone. You have to head out with fear and insecurities, without that cushion to fall back on. You must have some courage to make those mistakes and be ready for all that "I told you so."

This chapter is not against the family. I love mine quite unconditionally, but I cannot live my life according to their understanding of life. Fortunately, they have left me alone for longish periods of time and I already have developed a mind of my own. I like to make my decisions, even if they turn out to be catastrophic or brilliant. At least I will have no one else to blame.

All I am trying to say is, there might come a time in your life when you will have to stand up to your family and call the shit out. If your self-worth is associated with their approval, or that friend or that boss, or every successful person you know, you won't be able to call it. You can, and should, seek advice or guidance. Everyone's life is different. Like Lord Krishna says, we cannot pass the test of life by copying anyone else's answers, as everyone's question paper is different.

What if you are different? You do not wish to settle down or have babies or do a job or buy a house, or you wish to have a very regular life while your family comprises of hippies and artists. You should be able to choose your own ingredients of life: your own spices and sauces to make your favourite dish, as you will be swimming in this sauce for a long time to come. Your family is not at fault, as all families are inherently protective and somewhat restrictive. You have to detach your self-worth from them and return them all the unconditional love you have for them. Then you can paint your own 'Sun' in the sky.

Affirmation: I have unconditional love for my family, but my self-worth is independent of their approval.

All my decisions are unaffected by my family's negative and restrictive beliefs.

FOR EVERY MINUTE YOU ARE ANGRY, YOU LOSE SIXTY SECONDS OF HAPPINESS – RALPH WALDO EMERSON

Self-Worth and the Dream Relationship

(The Wrong Pursuit of Happiness)

For the longest time, I thought once I had my dream relationship, I would be the happiest. Well, every time I got into one, I faced disappointment. It was like it was written on the door, "Come in, disappointments and negotiations are a part of adulthood. You are welcome." How does it feel when your dreams crash again and again? Terrible.

I just realised this so much later than I should have in life. But as soon as I did, I left everything and sat down to write this chapter. It's 9:51 pm on Wednesday, Oct 23rd, 2019, and I haven't had dinner yet. I wanted to put this on paper first. For so long, I have barked up the wrong tree for my happiness, and not one human or cat has told me, "Hey girl! This is the wrong tree; nothing atop it."

Ask people who are in their dream relationships. Ask them after some years, and no! Social media is not a good way to find that out. I am good at research, and I stalked some really happy couples online (keep it shushed as if you haven't). So, either they are faking it, or they both are just happy people themselves and just happened to meet. It never happens that they were miserable, and they met, and voila, their life became dream-like. No. Well, I can hear you sigh, even if I wish it were true. Sadly, but truthfully, if you are unhappy, you are most likely to meet someone unhappy. It is a simple vibrational equation. You need to figure out a way to your happiness first.

I am not saying that you shouldn't dream, but do not put so much dreamy pressure on your prospective relationship. You will have a bad wake-up call from reality otherwise. Rather, dream of a happy life filled with things that make you happy. Dream of being happy, joyful and ecstatic, sans relationship.

Relationship # Happiness

(Happy You = Happy Relationships)

We have all been fed a lot of drama since we opened our eyes. The romantic movies of our country and the books on romance have been feeding us a lot of nonsense and unrealistic things. Do you really need so much drama in your life? Well, ordinary can be beautiful too. You don't have to become a vampire or convert a Casanova's heart, and what not to get there. This is not your full-time job like the ladies in those movies. How many of them have thriving careers? Or do you wish to open a morality school to change the person you meet? You can just find someone nice and sorted. Kindly check where you are getting the inspiration for your dreams from. I hope not from dubious sources or wrong beliefs of your family to find someone tall, beautiful, rich and what not (what if they are asshats). There is nothing wrong with being tall or pretty, but those criteria are not important for a long-term relationship.

So, rewrite your dream! True love is usually very different from what you imagine and, it's mostly by chance. Let go of your useless criteria and be open to beautiful possibilities in your life. Please be with someone for the right reasons. When you write your dream, make space for your goals and priorities too. Don't become the sacrificial lamb for your dream relationship, because now *Sati* is abolished. You will have to live with that regret if the dream crashes. My dream will come true with someone who actually asks me what makes me happy and knows what makes him happy. No one has asked me this question yet. Can you imagine!

P.S., I still dream of someone who agrees with pets because I always need animals in my life. They make me really happy (non-negotiable).

And someone who cooks me gourmet meals (negotiable).

Affirmation: My dream partner is someone who is right for me in every way and helps me realise my dreams.

FRIENDSHIP IS A SINGLE SOUL DWELLING IN TWO BODIES – ARISTOTLE

What is Wrong with Being Single?

It's the 3rd of May 2021, and I have this question popping in my head: why are we so against being single?

I have been miserable in my life because frankly, it is a tad bit easier to be miserable in a relationship. Being miserable individually is tough, despite that we don't wish to be single. We choose relationships, how much ever miserable they may be because they cover up other voids of our lives in the short-term. It does provide a distraction and gives us some breathing space or relief. That is why even the possibility of a relationship or a connection with someone makes us feel better.

Be miserable for some time. Be single and revel in your misery, then you will be able to solve your problems. Because in the long run, a wrong relationship can make you much more miserable, trust me! Solve your effing problems first.

Affirmation: I can be single till I find the right one.

BE BRAVE. TAKE RISKS. NOTHING CAN SUBSTITUTE EXPERIENCE – PAULO COELHO

Self-Worth and Looks

A thing of beauty is a joy forever, but the problem is we are not things.

We all have read this story in our childhood. Mirror, mirror on the wall, who's the fairest of them all? As a result, we all channel Cinderella's evil stepmother at some point in our lives. Now you can deny it all you want, but if you are threatened by or jealous of someone's looks, that is what is happening.

Why was she evil? She just wanted to look better than everyone else. Don't you? She just went a little overboard. When we are measuring ourselves as per external beauty with others, we are essentially doing the same. Is it your fault? No, it's the fault of your conditioning. When you are complimented too many times on your external features, they become part of your identity, and you obtain a sense of pride. And then when someone tells you your flaws, you feel bad. So, you are always yo-yoing like this.

The obsession with how we look vis-à-vis others and the insecurity that comes along result in associating our self-worth with looks. It is absolutely the stupidest way to measure yourself. Some of you might object that you do not do it. But ask yourself, if putting on an extra ten pounds or losing ten pounds makes you feel worse, not health-wise but emotionally. There you go. It covers everything, your looks, your weight, your complexion and your dressing sense. In the end, it matters very little. Why do they say happy girls are the prettiest? Have you ever noticed that you look better on a day when you are happy than on a day when you are sulking?

We are measured by society and the other gender on such scales, so they seem important. But tell me honestly, though, would you be with someone who only likes you for the way you look? How long can that last, and how happy will you be in that relationship? When you are in love with someone, do you constantly compare them to others? No, Right?! So, give your body the same kind of love. Love it truly and unapologetically. Take care of it and nurture it.

So, someone once asked me that if we don't measure ourselves with external benchmarks, then won't we feel a little bit empty; we wouldn't dress up anymore or be happy about looking good. I am not telling you to give it all up. Dress all you want and don't forget to accessorise! Do enjoy yourselves now that you are on earth, but stop taking it so seriously. So what if you become a little pudgy or thin, or have a pimple or two? You are so much more than that. When you walk into a room full of people, do you only get attracted to the best-looking person or the person who looks perfect? The matters of the heart, the heart only knows, whether you are attracted to someone or not. It has pretty much nothing to do with looks, I feel.

So please stop comparing yourself with others and focus on the right things. Be kinder, more compassionate. Let love flow through you. Be strong, accept and love yourself fully, and then tell me if you don't glow. You are beautiful already – Munsiyari, 22nd April 2019.

Affirmation: My self-worth is unattached to the way I look.

REMEMBER, BEAUTY CANNOT GET YOU LOVE, BUT LOVE CAN GET YOU BEAUTY – PRIYANNSHA

20 Pounds Heavier

When I opened my eyes, lol, just kidding. When I was in my twenties, I realised that I was 20 pounds heavier than the average woman around me. It made me very unhappy, and I felt that life was being unfair to me. I totally ignored the good things about me and attached my whole energy to those 20 pounds. I dieted, I exercised, and I lost them sometimes by falling sick. Whenever that happened, I felt amazing, beautiful and confident, but it came back though, and when that happened, I felt guilty and somewhat lesser.

I looked really good, sorry for the narcissism. I was gorgeous. People around me constantly kept telling me to lose those extra pounds, and then I would look so much better. After a point, I just wanted to slap them really and scream and throw a fit. And just say, I would if I could, you asshole.

I thought, somehow, if I lost these extra pounds, I would be at peace. It's Absolute crap! I'll tell you. So, I kept playing tug-of-war with these 20 pounds for a long period. I became very fragile about this. Now that I think of it, I ask myself why I make such a big deal out of it. I really cannot fathom why. Maybe you also have that one thing you obsess about your body, and if not, lucky you. Then my partner left me for someone who was 20 pounds lighter than me, hehe. I do laugh now, but it crushed me then. On top of that, someone said to me that maybe he left you because you put on weight. Why am I sharing this down-in-the-drain, rock-bottom story with you? Be patient! So, I damned those extra 20 pounds. I blamed them as my self-worth took a nosedive into an endless abyss of darkness. I am quite dramatic like that.

I did figure out later, that I had an autoimmune disease, and those 20 pounds were my body's backup plan to save my life in case of a relapse. It was my safety net. Those 20 pounds were trying to save my life. So, I learnt to love them and loved myself more. I learnt to love every inch of this gorgeous, fully functional body that can hike mountains and do whatnot. I worked on myself and my health. My autoimmune disease went away, and so did the pounds. I made it such a matter of pride that I never realised the source of the problem. If I had the chance to go back, I wouldn't waste a second on it and utilise that time to do something I love.

So, after I lost those pounds in 2020, I broke both my ankles one after the other, and the pounds came back. It can happen. Now, when someone tells me I have put on weight or lost weight, I smile. Sometimes I also laugh, depending on my mood, really. Why? Because I am enjoying my freedom. "I am much more than this," I want to tell them, but I would rather utilise that time doing something better.

P.S. Now I have grey hair, and I mostly don't colour it. It's driving people crazy. I am using my grey hair for further research and recording people's reactions to ageing. They are falling right into my trap.

Affirmation: My self-worth is unattached to my body size and body weight.

THE REAL ORNAMENT OF A WOMAN IS HER CHARACTER – MAHATMA GANDHI

Self-Worth and Saying No

You would think that when your self-worth increases, you will be saying YES to everything. It's exactly the opposite of that. I find myself saying NO much more, all the time, to many people across the board.

I realised I would say yes to many things before, some small, some big, like even moving to another country when I really wasn't sure. I even went on a trip with people I wasn't comfortable with. We all do things like these to be more likeable, or more acceptable to others. Now I have no such needs as I really like my own self, and I am very clear on things that I like and dislike. I have amazing boundaries now. It might sound selfish, but I can do a lot more for people now, without compromising on my happiness. So, it's a win-win.

What is in it for you? Other people cannot take advantage of you anymore by playing on your vulnerability or feelings of being unloved or of being unworthy. You are not saying 'Yes' to everything based on this principle, which is shit actually: "I am not good enough, so I must do more for people so that they like me." (If you are not good enough, which is not true in most cases, but if you feel that, then do more for yourself.) Doing this will make your boundaries rock solid, and will make you unravel all your toxic relationships, and you can get out of them.

You would say now, "What's such a big deal about saying NO?" Try doing it for some time with people you have been saying YES to for a long time. You will know. But this exercise is an important test to determine where you are on this journey. If you find yourself saying YES to things you regret later, you need to CIRCLE back. Figure out if you are doing all the work for some people in your life, just so that you can have them or convince them to keep them in your life. STOP IT. Look inside. What is it that is driving you to behave like that? Where is this coming from? It is generally the fear of not being liked, being loved, or being alone.

Why am I lecturing and harping so much on it? Because I want you to be single and happy, not single and miserable. When you are single, and the fears are still there, you will be saying YES to unnecessary people and things all the time. By all means, say Yes to people who are always there for you, but not to everyone. When you are single, this wish to be liked is heightened a little bit. Anyway, it's impossible to be liked by everyone, and it is completely alright. You just must like yourself and it's easier than you think it is. Start by saying NO a lot. I mean it, a lot. Do not go to events you don't wish to. Do not do things you do not wish to. And when people come and tell you to put yourself out there, put cake on their faces, I did that. Really.

You do not need to get out there and get uncomfortable. You need to do things you like so that it makes you shine more. What you need to do is only to dissolve your blocks and fears to attract the right person. You need not only to be single but happy too.

EXERCISE:

- Say NO to one person/ thing/ activity every day for a month.
- Write a list of things you said yes to (Big or small) and later regretted, as many as you want, FORGIVE yourself for them. E.g., I did a fake wedding with my husband, lol—this story is for one of my future books.
- Find out the fears that make you say YES to things that later make you unhappy. Write down all of them and BURN that paper, symbolically letting go of all these fears.
- Like and treat yourself for saying NO to things you would have said YES to before. Buy yourself a flower or a plant, or something you love. Be happy for yourself.

Affirmation: I never do anything that makes me uncomfortable in a negative way. I can say NO when that happens.

OPINION IS THE MEDIUM BETWEEN KNOWLEDGE AND IGNORANCE – PLATO

Self-Worth and Societal Standards of Material Success

Well, if I say that I have never been swayed by societal standards of material success, I would be lying.

I have dreamt at some point of things that are the epitome of social success, like the corner office, that car, that massage chair, the drop-dead gorgeous guy and so on. So, the issue with these is that they are achievable if you work hard enough, but how much joy they will bring you is questionable. It can be great or disastrous. The drop-dead gorgeous guy can be kind of a jerk, and the corner office can come with high blood pressure. I still would like the massage chair and maybe a nice car, don't see anything wrong with that. Just kidding, it can be great, your corner office and your gorgeous guy can be a dreamboat. See, I have no problem with your dreams, but I have problems with setting the same standards of success for everyone.

If someone asks me what is your dream company? I would say myself. I like my own company, after all. Gotcha. Also, going to the office every day at 8 am is not my idea of success. And what is this obsession with being a morning person? I like to write and contemplate at night. Why do I have to change my personality forcefully to become successful? I do not understand it.

My idea of success is doing very little work while earning a lot of money, and I am working towards it. How? It's not in this book. Do I wish to have a corner office in my dream company? Maybe it is a means to an end, but what I truly want is a home office with a pool. I would like to have enough money to do whatever the hell I wish to do with my life. Now you will say it's everyone's goal in life. First of all, that is not true. Some people love their jobs and offices. Great for them! Secondly, people who do not love their jobs and what they are doing with their lives have no clarity, and they get deeply stuck in those lifestyles. Why? Because they are following societal standards of success. I am following my own, so my probability of getting there is higher.

Living in apartments with high rents—almost 1/3 of your salary is gone. Then the fancy cars and home loans, because they are paying high rents, and they wish to buy a house. Also, they want to show off their success, so they further buy a lot of stuff they absolutely do not need just to prove to others and also to themselves how successful they are. It's completely idiotic in my eyes.

Okay, sometimes you have to get that job as a means to an end but do not get stuck in jobs or relationships due to money or any other wrong reason, except if it is your dream come true. To build a life which makes you feel truly successful, you have to go through this process of giving up on societal standards of success, or you will be playing catch-up all your life. There can be flashes of achievements and accomplishments and even some happiness in the midst of it, but inner peace is totally lacking in this process. Inner peace is the secret ingredient for the soup of true success.

So first, you must be at peace with your life, with what you want, and you should know what makes you happy. You get the gist. Then you evade all these traps and hustle to build your own life. So whatever path you take, be very sure of the end goal. Do not, I repeat, do not get caught up in the race. We are all running alone, remember that. You might not need that massage chair, but I do. I don't want to live in a posh apartment because I don't even like apartments. But I need to travel for my soul, and I need to be surrounded by plants and nature. Do I need a big car? I haven't decided that yet. You have to recognise what you need and avoid getting trapped in this "One plan for all". It will be great for you in the long run.

See, when you are free of these standards, you can use your time, money and resources to build your life the way you want. That will be the sweet-ass life that will make you truly happy. Even if you take a safer and slightly longer route of taking up a job and building it on the side, it's alright. As long as you are racing alone, you will be fine.

Affirmation: My self-worth is unaffected by societal standards of material success.

I am only competing against myself.

ENJOY EVERY MINUTE OF LIFE. NEVER SECOND GUESS LIFE – MICHAEL JORDAN

Then Came the One... Or So I Thought

After I wrote the major half of this book, my chest was all puffed, and I was feeling very proud of myself to be able to reach this level of self-love, self-nurturing and every aspect of self-worth, or so I thought. I was ready again to not be single. The universe laid the perfect trap. For one day, that one day I will regret the times to come, when I went on an online dating app, and I met him. He was like a breath of fresh air. Oh yes, I am a hopeless romantic if I haven't told you that before. That's why it was so difficult for me to be single—I love all the shenanigans that come with love and relationships.

Anyway, I met him, and let's call him Aqua because of his eyes (they were kind of green maybe). So, he was positive, intelligent, accomplished and blah blah. Now what else can you want? I don't know if Aqua will ever read this book, but he did not value me or respect me, and it made me so angry. I was irritated, frustrated, angry, and emotionally upset. I had already worked on myself for two years at that point, for two full years. I had high self-worth. I was blaming the Universe, blaming him and blaming everything and everyone. This incident made me forget the basic premise of self-work. (It happens to the best of us; that's why I hate love stories, well, sometimes.) LOOK INSIDE! Yes, that is the only solution at times like these. You must ask yourself some tough questions. You have work left to be done, and that's what the Universe is telling you. It's not Aqua's fault, it's yours, black. (insert your own eye colour). And boy, did I have work left. That was in the middle of 2019, and I was just starting to clear my ancestral and family beliefs, and it took me a solid three years or more.

So, I looked inside after having thrown a fit, of course. Then I calmed the fuck down. I asked myself if "I value myself enough"? What makes me value myself? What is the composition of my self-value equation? The best is to draw; you can draw your own. You must actually.

Self-value → Looks → How much I earn? → Relationships → Acceptance and appreciation from others → Acknowledgement of my achievements

These are the things that made me value myself. At that point, I was struggling with quite a few of these. Now the question is that if we don't link our self-value to these, what do we link it to? Always remember you were born a human being, so even if you twiddle your thumbs and do nothing, your energy imprint still has its own value. You can do a lot of course, but only telling you there is no need to link your value to these external factors at all. You are valuable to the Universe. It is a very basic concept that you should understand. You will alter the Universe by not being here. Whenever you start losing your value, just imagine you could have been an earthworm. In this web of life, you have a role to play, and everything external is very transient. So, linking your value to it is like losing your heart at losing a small competition compared to the big game. The big game is still there to be won.

So, when I met Aqua, I had nothing in the above diagram as per my definition. I was going through a transition phase. I valued myself as kind of low. Don't get depressed on my account.

Low self-value equals a guy who does not value you. BAM! One rookie mistake and three months of suffering in the middle of writing this book. This is the Universe keeping me humble or in check till I complete the work, I suppose.

P.S. So if you get into a relationship before you have worked on yourself, all you get is suffering. I valued myself at that point and told Aqua to leave. Also, I think I like black eyes much more.

Affirmation: I value myself highly, irrespective of what I own or achieve.

I value myself highly, irrespective of whatever I earn at a given point.

CHANCE IS A WORD VOID OF SENSE; NOTHING CAN EXIST WITHOUT A CAUSE – VOLTAIRE

Self-Worth and You
Defining Your Success

We as a society have become extremely vain, me included. We want constant compliments, we want to look good, and we want to have everything we set our eyes on. As partners, we want someone who wants the exact same materialistic things we are running after. We want friends who make us look good somehow. 'Perfect picture of social success' is what we wish to portray to other people. Is it making us feel good? We have put ourselves in a whirlpool of unending and unachievable goals, in which we keep going round and round.

A house, a car, a better-looking half and even friends who make you look good are not enough. We constantly compare ourselves to others who are even in bigger whirlpools. Earn more, spend more, go on better vacations, buy bigger cars and wear designer clothes. I have done that too. There is no problem with enjoying what you have. The problem is that when you go down the road picking up these small pebbles of temporary happiness, there is no time to realise whether you are going in the right direction or not. You are always busy doing this and that. Between work and fun weekends, time passes quickly, and we tend to put everything under the rug.

Fortunately, at a point in my life, I did have some time to introspect. I was mostly successful in worldly terms, but it was getting more and more difficult, as it really wasn't the path I wanted to tread. If you want a bigger car, great. But if I don't want it, why should I run after it? And let me tell you, it is not easy to step out of this race, because the moment you step down from this escalator, which is so fiercely woven in this society, you will be shaken a little bit. It's a given.

You will be judged a lot not only by others, but also by yourself. As you must have realised already that this book is not so much about others as it is about you. You will judge yourself a lot. We can easily deal with others, but if you think you are a failure, well, you definitely are. What I am saying is that you will have to change your beliefs, which you have been taught and which you have learnt or seen. "Artists don't make money", where did I learn that from? I don't even remember, but I did believe in it until I didn't anymore.

Once you unlearn that, you will realise that nothing you learnt was that important. Nothing you think will make you feel successful does. So, stop judging yourselves and being so harsh on yourselves. Even if you have two fewer shoes or a smaller car, who cares? Only you, maybe, but you should not. The easiest way to measure it is, for six months of your life, don't engage in social validation of what you do. Like if you buy a new dress, don't tell anyone. You go on a trip, don't put it on social media.

No one will miss you. Don't worry. I am just separating your happiness from social validation. This exercise will help you really find out what gives you that feeling of accomplishment. It might be drastically different, or it might be the same. For example, you may not be happy with investment banking, and you may wish to become a social media influencer. Do try it.

See what will happen when you self-realise or know what success means for you. Will you become overly successful overnight? Probably not, but you will make efforts in the right direction. And you won't care so much about stuff that is not important.

P.S. While doing this exercise of success realisation, a lot of people will leave your life. You will trigger them in the wrong way, but they are just jerks. Good people will stick. Don't care about the ones who leave.

Affirmation: I will build a life that is desirable to me.

YOU MAY FIND YOUR WORST ENEMY OR BEST FRIEND IN YOURSELF – ENGLISH PROVERB

Ladders X Gardens

I remember a conversation between one of my ex-bosses and me. I told him I wished to become a consultant, the day someone gave me a consulting job, and he said, don't we all hope for that? Is it true, though? I couldn't see him doing a consulting job. He loved to Lord over everyone in the office, so much so that he was always in the office and barely went home. Does everyone wish for the same things? I refuse to believe that. Some people are ambitious in a worldly way; me not so much. My idea of success does not include slogging my ass off for twelve to fourteen hours in an office. I started missing sunsets, which is my favourite time of the day. Does that mean I am lazy or a shirker? Absolutely not. I just want different things. I am a creative soul, so I like to ideate and create. Frankly, if success happened by just working hard, then our farmers would be the most successful. They toil so hard but are struggling to thrive.

People are constantly telling me to work really hard to achieve anything in life.

Unfortunately, I cannot work too hard. It stresses me out. Do not judge me. I am smart, and I like to work in my own way. I randomly indulge in creative activities, which is also hard work but doesn't feel like it. I can write for hours, but it doesn't feel like hard work. Not at all, and I will love a job where I have creative freedom. You bet. Coming back to the recipe for success If I had listened to everyone's suggestions, I would be stuck just doing things for money. 'Work hard and earn money' is the mantra, right? No judgment here, if the corporate ladder of success excites you and making money drives your ass out of bed; if your blood is blue or your collar, for that matter, go for it. But remember, don't judge others who have a different picture of success. We are all supposed to be different. Even having a beautiful child or being a homemaker could count as being successful if the person involved is happy doing it. For some people, making enough money to survive but having a lot of time on their hands makes them feel successful. Who are we to judge or push anyone? For someone, buying an Audi can feel like a success. The main issue here is allowing others to define it for you and putting others down who do not follow the same path. Don't let even your family define it for you.

If you are unhappy, stop doing what you are doing. Break the cycle of monotony to pause and reflect. Write down your roadmap to success. I will share mine here, but it's subject to change:

1) To have a small garden.
2) To be able to write.
3) To be able to have pets.

4) To have at least one child.
5) To be able to get a massage weekly / fortnightly.
6) To be able to watch sunsets with a cup of tea (very important for Vitamin D levels)
7) To have loving friends/family who wish me well and are as happy for my successes as I am for theirs.
8) To have an interesting social life with a lot of fun activities.
9) Travel frequently enough to satisfy the cravings of my soul.
10) To have a hair stylist on call (aspirational)
11) To have a Personal assistant (very aspirational)
12) To have true love (very, very aspirational but non-negotiable)
13) To have money to do whatever the hell I want and go after my dreams.
14) Perfect health.

Anyway, I suggest in life, do not wait, and do not make it too late to find out what makes you feel that you have arrived. Don't look at Sharma *ji ka beta* or that cousin who everyone has (eye roll). Do not run after goals which are not even yours. Make a list of your own.

P.S. I love making lists.

P.S. II: If you take a break in your career, the sky will not fall on you. You are allowed to do it and contemplate. Don't worry, you can recoup later. I love Mini retirements.

Affirmation: I can build my own road map to success without external judgments influencing me.

WHAT IS CALLED GENIUS IS THE ABUNDANCE OF LIFE AND HEALTH – HENRY DAVID THOREAU

Self-Worth and Friends

This is the most unexpected chapter of this book, for me, I mean. I have always prided myself on having an excellent set of friends. So, when I started to work on myself, I was expecting claps, whistles and confetti. But, I got judgment, weird statements and a lot of isolation. I am sharing this with you because once you start on this journey of self-worth, you will be prepared.

The moment you start to come into your own, unlock your creativity and start changing for the better, you will create shifts in your relationships. At that point, it is most likely you will get hurt. I advise you to be an observer and let it happen. Then there will be some who will think you are super weird but will stick around. Keep them.

Let's start from the top. Half of my friends left the moment I stopped drinking. I do drink an occasional glass of wine even now, but it is occasional in the true sense. So essentially, these are the **Socialisers.** These are rats on your ship; they leave as soon as the party leaves. Instead of appreciating me for taking care of my health, they called me old and boring. Well, I would rather be boring than unhealthy. So much so for peer pressure for alcohol. I have never been so pressured by friends or acquaintances to do something right. It brings me to the conclusion that they want you to be stuck in the same place where they are stuck. Leaving alcohol brought a lot of new things and adventures in my life. I think it made my life much more interesting. I have no judgment against it, but we should not force anyone to make their life choices based on our hobbies or likes. I say do not be afraid to break away from something you have wanted to do just because of social reasons as better things await you.

When I decided to take a break for my spiritual practice and to meditate, a lot of people told me to get back to a job. I call them the **Normalisers.** They want you to be as normal as possible, whatever their definition is. They exhibit signs of shallow talk, insecurities and self-worth issues. They are more dangerous because they don't leave you, and you must leave them. Otherwise, they will constantly project their self-worth issues onto you.

So, when suddenly the Socialisers and Normalisers are gone, you will be left alone for some time. Here you will learn the lesson of Solitude and how being alone can be better than bad company. It is an important life lesson, for being able to stand alone in your truth. People who actually want to see you grow in life will stay, but they will be far and few. After a while, when you have spent some time alone, a beautiful thing will happen. You will attract new people. Be patient, they will surely come, and some of the older ones will rise to the occasion and will come back. So, do not stop your journey for fear of losing friends. If they are truly your friends, you will not lose them in the first place. The Rest is baggage which needs to be left behind. This new category is what I call "FRIENDS", really. They will be true to themselves and to you. They will grow with you and will help you grow, too.

There are some other categories also:

- Complainers
- Emotional Victims
- People who refuse to look inside
- People who feel they are wronged by everyone
- People who love to discuss growth but do zilch essentially.

All the above people are essentially nice people. But you need to decide where you want to put your energy in the name of friendship and company. Like I always say, "Be kind, not Stupid". I rest my case here.

P.S. When you unlock your creativity and/or spirituality, you will trigger everyone whose creativity/ spirituality is unlocked. So do not share too much or be prepared for major backlash. Do not try to make them understand, as it's not the time for them yet.

Affirmation: I attract friends I deserve in my life who are positive for me and cheer me on while I slay my goals one after another.

NO INDIVIDUAL CAN WIN A GAME BY HIMSELF
— PELE

Self-Doubt as a Partner in a Relationship

For a long ass time, people kept asking me, "How come you are still single?"

I usually say I am waiting for the one who deserves me, as I have worked on myself so much that I cannot be in a relationship with just anyone. However, inside I felt uneasy. It was the truth, then why? I always carried this nagging feeling that I was not good enough for a partner, or for any relationship. My self-doubt cropped in whenever I met someone; maybe he could do better, find someone better looking, or someone who would sacrifice more, or someone who is more giving (I am already too giving). I doubted myself if I was the best possible choice for that relationship, hence I also doubted the other person. I projected my self-doubt on them completely. If someone has chosen me, I must be the best for him, and if I choose someone, clearly, he should be the best for me.

If we are comparing ourselves and our partners and our relationships to other people's, where does it end, really? There is no end to this; I can do better, or my partner can do better. To get the partner we deserve, first, we need to work on ourselves to make ourselves a total catch (not In the way you think). I worked on myself to imbibe the qualities my partner should have: Success, kindness, honesty, courage, emotional strength, health/fitness, mental strength and patience (this was the toughest one for me). I got really impatient in relationships. I really needed to calm the fuck down to make sane decisions, and not get too excited too soon when I meet and like someone. So first, I removed my own self-doubt and then became what I wanted from the other person. Also, I had to let go of all social conditioning of how my partner should be, as I wanted my partner to like me the way I am. Well, I had to extend the same courtesy to him.

I feel expecting someone to have all the things you lack is going to create a juxtaposition, which you might not like. Yes, opposites attract. I can hear the rebellious voices, but that doesn't come from a place of lack. So, make yourself '*Qaabil*' enough before judging the other. Also, to find a vibrationally compatible match, you kind of have to be at the same level in every way, more or less. So, you don't have to be monetarily equally successful, but you both must think of yourself as successful and emit that vibration. I also do not mean that you should be cloned or have the same hopes and dreams. What I mean is that a kind person will attract a kind person, and a patient person will attract a patient person, barring karmic relationships. So, I made a list! I like making lists, as you know. I started to work on myself. There were personal and professional goals to be met so that I am ready to receive the one I deserve. Now, when it happens, I can say, I have earned it.

Affirmation: I am a divine gift for my partner. My partner is lucky to have me.

THE FLOWER DOESN'T DREAM OF THE BEE. IT BLOSSOMS AND THE BEE COMES – MARK NEPO

Angry Bird

I went to Goa for my friend's bachelorette and somehow got left alone one day in the middle of North Goa (not in the middle of nowhere). It made me angry. My friend—we are still friends—who is a really good sport and knows me quite well, coined the term that day. She was trying to placate me and said, "My angry bird." I totally refuted it, of course.

Years later, when I started to work on myself, I realised I indeed did get angry over the silliest of things. Anger that is always triggered by other people's behaviour is nothing but a lack of self-worth. I wanted everything to go my way. I wanted to control almost every situation in life. It never goes like that, and you just stay perpetually angry. There are times when anger is justified, but more often than not, it's not, and mine wasn't. It is not that easy to accept this; even tougher to find that about yourself. I had to do a lot of digging under my jovial, happy social surface to find out that I had the properties of an angry bird. Sometimes what others can easily see takes us a long time to find out.

So, I decided to become a nice singing canary from that point. I found out the triggers that made me angry. I had to be silent, get insulted many times, not respond and just observe what all makes me angry. The turning point of this whole exercise was when I accepted that I was an angry person, so that I could remove all my triggers.

I had all these kingly expectations, God only knows why, where I wanted others to say yes, all the time, to listen to me all the time, to almost like follow my orders and do what I wished them to do. I sound horrible, but it was worse. Now combine impatience and emotions, and voila, a potent combination for disaster. It resulted in underlying seething anger, which completely spoiled my health.

Nothing saps your energy like 'Anger', I am telling you. Maybe I was some king in one of my past lives (just kidding), but not in this life for sure. Now, you may ask what my self-worth has got to do with it. Well, if your self-worth is intact, you do not care how others behave with you. They can ignore you or do anything, but it does not affect you. The desire to control others can affect your relationships majorly, or you yourself. Angry birds are only good in video games. Neither do you wish to be one, nor do you want one in your life.

P.S. After I removed my triggers, my life became quite boring. All the drama reduced considerably, and I didn't spend time thinking about how badly behaved everyone around me was. I suddenly had too much time on my hands. I was having withdrawal symptoms, and missing my anger, but I chose less drama, as my gut got so much better.

For your reference, My triggers are:

- When someone said NO to me.
- When someone ignored me.
- When things didn't go as planned.
- When someone disrespected me.
- When God won't listen to me and won't give me what I wanted (I didn't even spare him).

Hopefully, you got the gist... now find out your own triggers and get to work. Chop Chop.

Affirmation: I honour all my emotions, including the negative ones like anger.

IT ALWAYS SEEMS IMPOSSIBLE UNTIL IT'S DONE
– NELSON MANDELA

The Heart Wants What the Heart Wants

I say this a lot, whenever someone asks me: Why are you doing this? Are you not afraid? Does it even exist? How do you manage to do it? You are delusional, crazy, impractical, blah, blah, blah. I just say the heart wants what the heart wants.

My heart has wanted many things over the years, but nothing more than true love. Was it the effect of all the love stories, Korean soap operas or the fairytales I have seen and read all my life? Maybe that, but don't we all want it? I believe God made all the suffering, and then he made love. He sent us on earth to learn lessons, and he must have thought the question paper that I have set is too hard. Let me give them some grace. Let me show them some love, even if they don't deserve it. Though being God, he tied it up with heartbreak and lessons, but we still cannot give it up, and we should not. The biggest sufferings and failings vanish when the person we love smiles at us. It truly amazes me.

So, the heart wanted true love, but it eluded me. I had experiences, feelings, emotions, and heartbreaks, but I am unsure if I have experienced true love. Then one day, when I was all ready to shut shop and close my heart because I got all tired of waiting. I am also human like they say. It dawned on me that only when I have truly loved myself can I love another. Maybe I have also never truly loved anyone. And the funny thing about the Universe is, if your heart really wants something, it doesn't keep it from you. It will make you work, make you cry, make you howl, but you will be led to it. The question is, how much do you really want it? You can't act all intelligent and suave, but you have to act like a total fool. You have to refuse to listen to logic. People might hurt you while you are looking for what you want. Let them, it's just part of the process. Just because they have not known it, does not mean it does not exist. You have to go on this journey alone to find whatever you want. It can be love or it can be peace, or it can be peaceful love. It can be anything you desire. You just can't stop believing in it, even for a minute.

I asked for true love, and I had to change for that. I had to look inside and accept everything about me. I had to love myself truly first. Not the kind where I eat junk food and watch TV all day long because I love myself. I had to care truly about myself. I had to love my smile as much as I loved another's.

And when you find that love with yourself, the heart becomes full and doesn't long for anything. Everything dims in comparison. It is called true love for oneself. It is like, whatever you want, you become that. You not only find it, but you also become it. You become love! And if you are love, what will you attract? Duh .

So become what your heart wants.

Affirmation: I will make heart-based decisions, even if others can't see the why of it.

I will make decisions that make me happy because I love myself.

PERSEVERANCE IS FAILING 19 TIMES AND SUCCEEDING THE 20TH – JULIE ANDREWS

Self-Love and Addictions

For the longest time, I claimed to love myself a lot, and I hid all my unhealthy behaviour, patterns and addictions under that claim of self-love. I picked up smoking, God knows why. I drank myself to death every weekend because I loved myself. I fell in love again and again! Was that because I loved myself, or was I stupid? I was just addicted to it, I guess.

"Self-love" is an over-abused term; we have started using it loosely. It should be replaced with "tough self-love", really. Taking it easy and putting everything under the rug is not self-love. Harbouring unhealthy addictions is self-harm, not love, so stop calling it that.

I had to process a lot of things and change them while writing this book. Honestly, I don't preach what I cannot apply to myself. Otherwise, it just wouldn't ring true. It will not hit you the way it should if it is not written with absolute honesty. My worst addictions were not any substances, but bad relationships and boy, can they be addictive. One after the other! I just couldn't stay single. And whatever I thought was making me socially acceptable and apparently cool was all leading to self-harm. So, when you start doing this exercise, you might need to pause for some time because you will have to reconsider your entire lifestyle. Do it one by one; not together; it's hella tough.

I started with the substances. Next, I controlled my unnecessary shopping. Really, I was a hoarder, and it was affecting my savings. I wasn't able to invest in things I really wanted to do. Then I left sugar. This was the toughest; I had crazy withdrawal symptoms. So, I switched to jaggery sugar. I felt I was dying. I didn't care if it was effective or not). After that, I deleted my Netflix account, or this book would not have existed.

If you are already like a super disciplined person and you don't need all this *gyaan*, then you can move to the next chapter. But whatever your addictions are, may be super disciplined, I would like you to look at them once and then consider if it is going to harm you in the long run or destroy your balance. I am also addicted to my work, so I don't have enough balance there. Anything that gives you instant gratification is usually not self-love, like talking to that person who is wrong for you. You can make exceptions sometimes. I have a glass or two of wine occasionally, but I do not drink, sleep and repeat every weekend anymore. If you think that if you change, your life will suck and it will get boring, it is not true. Let me tell you what happened to me.

Let's make a list of my favourite things which I gave up:

- Alcohol:
    a. Saved a lot of money.
    b. Travelled much more.

c. Engaged in productive weekends.
d. Got better skin, hair and sleep.

- Netflix:
  a. Read a ton of books and created a YouTube series on books.
  b. Started painting again.
  c. Meditated a lot. (You can always borrow someone's Netflix. I still watch movies online with my brother's account, what I am saying is don't waste all your free time on it) It should be a choice, not an addiction.
- Unhealthy eating:
  a. Joined the gym (just happened in sync).
  b. Got the glutes I always wanted.
- Bad relationships:
  a. Wrote this book with the time I saved from dating the wrong people.
  b. Picked up new hobbies like gardening, which I had no time for earlier.
  c. Spent time with animals and revelled in their unconditional love. It was the best time spent ever.

I was an easy prey to addictions. I was lazy, weak-willed, and generally quite casual about things. If you are not, it will be easy for you. I just switched my bad addictions to good addictions, as a part of my self-love quest. Why did I do it? Because I wanted to achieve great things in life and design a life I love. And I needed myself in the best shape and energy for that. That doesn't mean I didn't fail, I did, a lot. Then I reminded myself of the love I have for myself, and I didn't give up. I tried again till I turned things around. If you believe you can turn things around, You can.

Trust me, if I can do it, you can, and you will be so much better than me.

P.S. I am the black unicorn of my family. Black because I am the worst, Unicorn because I love myself, and I am magical.

Affirmation: I love myself too much to take on any negative addictions. I really take care of myself.

EXPERIENCE IS THE NAME EVERYONE GIVES TO THEIR MISTAKES – OSCAR WILDE

Self-Worth and Helping Others

Do you have this intense craving to help others, so much that you ignore yourself? Does it make you a better human being? For the longest time, I kept finding people I could help, my house help, my colleagues, and people I was dating. If I wasn't helping someone, it made me uncomfortable and unfulfilled. I helped even when others didn't ask for it. It completely took away my energy, and I was always tired.

Now, if we help others, we are termed as nice people. But helping others to feel fulfilled is also selfish; in fact very selfish. Also, what is even worse is obligating people by helping them and then later expecting them to help you back or acknowledge you. Trust me, it is a useless kind of cycle that you don't want to be a part of.

Much later, I found out that compulsively helping others is a cry for help for yourself. If you are helping others too much and going out of your way, you definitely want someone to help you. Help yourself first, and this intense need will go away. Of course, you can help, but not because you want to. When you tell yourself that you can help yourself, you will be more centred and happier.

After all, who is more worthy of your help than yourself? No one.

I have seen many people who are constantly helping others and are insanely good people, but they are ignoring their personal lives or goals or something else in the process. Life becomes a puzzle to them. Then they wonder, I am a nice person, and I am helping everyone, still, why is no one happy with me? Why are people ignoring my needs? It is because you are depriving yourself of that happiness, and you are ignoring yourself. You cannot grow materially or spiritually in deprivation. Even if you deprive yourself of one thing materially, your soul will bring you right back for that one thing.

By helping yourself, making yourself the utmost priority (in balance, of course, not narcissistically) and letting go of the obligation of helping others, you will move forward towards your purpose. You might end up helping hundreds or thousands or even a million people by just doing what you are supposed to be doing or just by being you. On top of that, you will be happy and fulfilled.

P.S. Your self-worth will not be calculated by how many people you helped. You are worthy as it is. Don't feel so pressured. Find your purpose — Saharanpur, Aug 11, 2019 (my ancestral home)

Affirmations: "I can help myself, but I gratefully receive any help that the Universe sends my way.

"I will follow my life purpose, and others will be helped by that without me going out of my way."

ACT AS IF WHAT YOU DO MAKE A DIFFERENCE. IT DOES – WILLIAM JAMES

Lack of Focus

We all have heard of the grocery list. We are constantly reminded of it by our neighbours and relatives. Find love by 25, get married by 30, have children within a year or two and own a house by 35. Nothing wrong if your #lifegoals are in sync, but it gets very tough for people like me, who are late at everything in life. I am scared of no one, except my mother's house help, who are really judgmental about me. Like recently, I was told by one of them that I should visit a gynaecologist as I needed to have babies like yesterday. Poor thing had no idea that I hadn't even found the man I would like to reproduce with, yet.

For a black unicorn like me, the list is very different. I want to be happy. (How dare I?). Well, I do want to get married, and I have once already, so technically do want to get married again, and have a family, but I am in no hurry. My list looks like this right now: buy a headphone, learn Spanish, learn Vedic astrology, and read the *Vedas*. And even if I put a husband on my list, he will come when he has to, not that he will materialise from thin air because I have exceeded the timeline.

So, I have been put in this box "lacks focus" by the other box of highly driven people. Listen to the ***Jame Rahon*** song, movie ***Taare Zameen Pe*** for reference. Well, highly driven people do everything by the clock and initially, life can seem richer and more successful. (These people have sharp edges.)

People who lack focus are flowing, with softer edges and abundant, if not necessarily richer. They usually take their time to decide what they want from life and blossom, but are usually more successful later on in life.

Again, coming back to myself. For the longest time, I couldn't figure out what I wanted to do with my life and what would make me happy. There was a certain void, a lack of fulfilment and envy, not with the highly driven, never. I was envious of those child prodigies; they knew what they wanted to be since they were toddlers. Here I was doing something in my late twenties, not really knowing what I wanted to do, except pay bills. I felt there was more to life than just paying bills and celebrating weekends. So, in my case, it was more of a "lack of life path or purpose."

When I asked people around me, they seemed miserable, too, and thus of no help. It's like we were all in a hamster wheel running nonstop, doing the same thing over and over every month. It wasn't that I hated my job—in fact, I was quite good at it, and I enjoyed what I did. I wanted more. There are things that you are good at, but there are things you love to do or are born to do. There are things which fill your pockets and pay your bills, and there are things which fill your soul and make your life worth living. If they are the same for you, you are one lucky bastard, but it doesn't have to be the same. Maybe you are an accountant, but you love to sing. Do not stop singing. You are a CEO, but you love photography. Never stop clicking. It is not just a hobby; it is your life force. Remember that.

If you think I will give you a motivational speech about leaving your job and pursuing your passion, I will not. I do not know about your life circumstances. I do not know if it is a wise decision for you. But I know if you have the courage and resources, do it. It is your life, and it has to be your decision. You can even fail at it, no Biggie. So, my friend, if you need that job right now, keep it. If it makes you feel safer, why not? But do not give up your dreams and your passions. Take your dreams seriously. Do not get into the race of buying and collecting things, unless that is your passion. You decide. I would just say plan the shit out of your life. Strive for your happiness. If you want to focus on something, focus on being happy and things that make you happy. The Rest is all transient, so no need to worry about it.

Coming back to my unique case. I am going to share it even if you are not interested. Why? Because I can. Let's not forget—I am the worst. I loved learning about unusual things and then writing about them. The missing gear of being overly driven and focused on that one job, one car and one house can be attributed to my immense curiosity about other things, which cannot be seen with the 'Naked-eye'. It was a blessing in disguise, or I wouldn't have learnt so much in life. This so-called lack of focus drove me into directions I would have never taken otherwise. I embraced that about myself. For the longest time, I kept wondering where my missing gear was and Why I was not driven like others. I wasn't here to participate in any race. I was here to observe and learn. Find out what you are here for, and please take your time. Let no one rush you, including yourself. You will find out when the time comes. Till then, enjoy the race or sit aside and eat snacks like me.

P.S. In between all this, I resigned to the fact that I have no special gift. But I rehired myself later. After all, in this case, you are your own boss.

Affirmation: I refuse to put pressure on myself just because others expect me to.

IF YOU HAVE NEVER FAILED, YOU HAVE NEVER LIVED – ABRAHAM LINCOLN

Self-Worth and Seeking Validation by Suppressing Emotions

The most important external factor for self-worth is validation from other people, and sometimes we get trapped in wanting to be validated for something which is not even our true personality or true self.

My parents and my relatives always kept complimenting me on how I am always calm and how I never get angry. So, as a child, I thought it was not alright to be angry and stopped accepting anger as an emotion. But, there is always a 'but'. Much later in my life, I realised that by not acknowledging my anger and reacting at the right moment, I became a ticking time bomb, and Boy, did I explode at all the wrong times. Also, to add a cherry on the cake, I couldn't forgive people easily, because for that, I first needed to get sufficiently angry with them. I was always doubtful about how I should react, as I thought they would not like me if I got angry. I needed to accept first the fact that I could get angry, and it would be okay. This is just one example of how we should not accept validation for suppressed emotions because as humans, we must exhibit these emotions. What we have to learn is how to deal with them and Not how to suppress them. Being in touch with your emotions is the first step to healing yourself.

We often lose ourselves when we try to please others and are they pleased like ever? Well, it's rare! So letting go of this need for validation is really important. Like Becca Lee said: "The surest way to lose your self-worth is by trying to find it through the eyes of others."

Self-worth and self-love come from accepting your, darker parts. I admitted to myself after the first half of my life that I had become angry, easily. Only then was I able to fix it. Otherwise, I would have committed to being this person who was so chilled out on the outside but seething inside. I would have remained unhappy.

P.S. What's with people telling women to be happy and to smile all the time? I was constantly told by some people to be happy during the worst phases of my life. If someone is happy in those circumstances, they are probably insane. You should run in the opposite direction from where these people are heading. Accept that you are unhappy in the first place. That is when things will start to shift.

Affirmation: "It is safe to accept my emotions.

"My self-worth is independent of external validation."

I TRIED TO DROWN MY SORROWS, BUT THEY LEARNED TO SWIM – FRIDA KAHLO

Daddy's Little Princess

We all have that one person in our lives who wants to validate us. Usually, that person refuses to see your ways, and the more they refuse to appreciate you, the harder you try. For me, it was my 'Father'. He was socially popular and quite successful, so I wanted to be like him at one point. I used to always hang out with my father when I was a child, and I found him really cool. But when I grew older, I found myself doing the exact opposite of what he told me, always. So we drifted apart.

It made me very sad to be misunderstood by him, and whenever I did anything for his validation, it didn't work. In fact, much later in life, I remember him telling me that I should have studied engineering. I was stumped. At the time, I was trying to thrive on my creative talents, making it even harder. He only wanted job security for me, not for any selfish reasons. He was only thinking of my best interests in his own way. But was being an engineer best for me? Hell No!

I always thought he would be proud of me, whatever I did. But I was a rebel, and he didn't like it. I chose my own relationships, which failed more often than they were successful. I did what I wanted, but I did want to hear " Well done," "You are so strong," or "I am proud of you." Alas, it was a far-fetched dream. Well, it never came as I was doing it all wrong, as per him, and it was making him very nervous.

I was a troublemaker in my parent's eyes. Why couldn't I do something noble, like become a doctor or an engineer? He even suggested becoming a lecturer. Why did I have to be so different and become a spiritual coach of all things? What does it even mean? He couldn't believe I was making my living by such unorthodox means. He would say "You did two MBAs." What about them? Are you kidding me? "What do you mean you cannot live with your husband anymore? You picked him."

Well, my sympathies in this case are with my parents. Imagine having a child like me. The issue is that my parents are too normal for me, and I am not at all normal for them. It was such a mismatch, I felt I was born in the wrong family. I was not doing it intentionally—I was just born different. But they had no clue about this finding your true self, and neither did they care. My father was very practical and grounded. I didn't care about my mother's approval because I never had it, but I was my father's favourite. My 'princess crown' was in danger. To him, I was speaking German. He thought I would turn out like Ariel, who sold her soul to a witch and then daddy had to rescue her. He doesn't read fairy tales, but something along those lines, I suppose.

In the end, there was no happy ending. But I decided to keep my crown intact. I have my ways. Well, I showed him my unconditional love for him, which will never change, whatever I do and with whoever I am. It will be a constant. Did he change? YES! He never said it, but I felt it. Also, I accepted his concerns and complaints as love, and I felt at peace. I let go of my validation problems and accepted that parents will be parents. I will let them worry a bit.

P.S. Also want to add this: Please gift this book to your friends so that I can justify writing this to my dad. He is going to ask me. How many people have read your book? Holding on to my crown with both hands and not vacating my throne like ever.

Affirmation: I will write my own fairy tale even if the people whom I love hold their approval, and it doesn't come easily.

I WISH TO LIVE A LIFE THAT CAUSES MY SOUL TO DANCE INSIDE MY BODY – DELE OLANUBI

Never Been Single

At age 35, I was able to write this chapter with great difficulty, as I had to wait to be single for a duration for at least a while before I was even qualified to write this. I have been single now for almost a year, and it has happened for the first time since I was 18 years old. Don't judge me, it included really long-term relationships, and my parents know about everything. In your face, you.

Sorry, I got carried away. Coming back to the chapter, I never got off the train of my failed relationships. We don't know where that train was heading, but not to a happy place, I suppose. When you place your happiness in someone else's hands, even if that man/woman is like half-hanging from a moving train to catch you (got the reference?), you are making a stupid decision. Don't do that.

So I can lie now and say that I love it. I am making great choices for myself and enjoying my freedom. It is far from the truth, I am not that put-together single person. I am in awe of them. My life is not a bed of roses from any angle. Imagine I am that person who loves being in a relationship so much that I don't even breathe before I run into another relationship. I take more breaths between my yoga poses. Why did I choose to be single then? Not for the lack of options (bragging much, this statement is based on crumble matches and hence has no basis or proof), but I got emotionally exhausted from being in the wrong ones. Phew, don't we all get exhausted by that? It was for breaking the patterns, which I refused to acknowledge. I lacked knowledge about myself to really be in a relationship or, to be honest, even BE. And it was damn tough for me to be single, I tell you.

I have been so busy just doing these relationships, which usually end up the same way. Tears and heartbreak. Some massive, some smaller. I wanted that connection, that one relationship. I don't think everyone seeks that kind of love, but I do. I need to have it. No judgments if you don't care about it. In my case, even if I have every material thing and do not have someone to share it with, I won't be completely happy. That's my reality, and I have accepted it. So I did what I needed to do. I went over all my wrong relationships. I healed, and forgave myself (really important) and others. I built a connection with myself. I really didn't know what I liked, but I do now. I always did what the other person liked and had this tendency to lose myself in a relationship. I ate chicken for 6 years, almost every day, and I hated eating chicken. When I figured it out, I realised my body and I like a completely plant-based diet. I watched too many late-night movies in one, and I don't like that. I like sleeping in and reading instead. It is not their fault, it is mine.

When I realised this, I made promises to myself, that I would be there for myself next time. I will take care of myself even if no one else does. I will love myself and trust me, no one can do it better than yourself. I will be happy on my own first. It is, of course, easier for you to know yourself and do it. Does that mean now I am against relationships? Not at all. Fixing your own relationship with yourself only guarantees better relationships, and not only romantic—all relationships of mine have elevated. Two empty vessels can only produce noise, while two happy people will multiply each other's happiness. I am no longer scared to be single. What scares the shit out of me is to be in a pointless ass relationship where I already know that person is not great for me. Why in the world will I do it? Or you do it? Well, it is a clear sign of low self-worth.

Also, when you start taking care of yourself, you start doing what you always wanted to do. I started doing impossible things, like sleeping on time and waking up on time (if only you knew me, you would know how impossible that is for me) and doing yoga I wrote this book with my full-time work, which was impossible under the relationship domino effect. I stopped waiting for someone to show up and started doing what I wanted. I would recommend that highly. Stop waiting, start doing your shizz. Shine wherever you are, do whatever you want, love your effing life even if you are single.

Never ever go into a relationship just for the heck of it. I did—this is a funny one—one fine day, I thought, why don't I just date someone for the heck of it? One friend, or rather a person, fixed us up. As you can imagine, with a totally wrong person for me. That is why I demoted them to a person from a friend. I dated him for 3-4 months. I have no clue in the world, why? Honestly, sometimes I do weird things. Like, he was nice and all, nothing against him. One fine day, he comes along and tells me, "I am not that into you." My pride/ego was a bit hurt, but frankly, my heart was dancing, I swear. I have never felt such mixed emotions in my life. Don't get into something you can't get out of. Totally grateful to that guy.

Please wait for the right person, don't be like me. Wait for flowers and violins, for the signs. Just kidding, grow up. Okay, maybe some flowers and some music and some butterflies at least. Wait for the one who is sweet and patient with you, not the knight or the princess in the shining armour. Maybe you will get someone who can cook, who likes animals, or even babies. Bonus if he is a good listener.

Most importantly, one who is totally into you, who is sure (give him time, of course) and is good for you, Is positive for you, roots for you, loves and encourages you to be yourself. Be single till then, it's perfectly okay. It has a lot of benefits, a lot of them. I wrote this chapter lying down in my bed, all to myself, eating my favourite snacks, and doing my favourite activity. Writing, of course, what else?

Okay, I realised I liked a lot of things when I was single, and I will tell you now. Why, we have been through this before because I can, and I am the worst. Swimming, growing flowers, painting, writing, drinking flower teas quietly without a peep, fountain pens, naps, bird watching, long walks, brunches that last forever, honest people, true friendships, dogs and cats, Sparkly little objects, fairy gardens, walking on the grass barefoot, rolled down windows on a road trip, road trips…

P.S. Imagine an alternate universe where being a couple is prohibited, you will be looked down upon and ostracised if you are with someone. Will you still be in this current relationship you are in and lose all the benefits? If your answer is NO, don't be in it.

Affirmation: I will get into a relationship only for the right reasons.

IF YOU FELL DOWN YESTERDAY, STAND UP TODAY – H. G. WELLS

Self-Worth and Relationships

We all judge ourselves for failed relationships. Abandonment and rejection are the toughest things to handle. How can we do it then? We all learn life lessons for success, but no one teaches us how to handle failure. Most relationships stem from a fear of being alone. You get into anything because of fear, how can it make you feel secure? Being alone requires more courage, so don't allow anyone to judge you. Most of us are in self-doubt, and out of fear of rejection, we put on a mask. We try to cover up what we think are our shortcomings and are steadfast in our projections. I think, vulnerability is required to really open up and have great relationships, even though all dating advice is against it. When we are not even being our real selves, how do we attract real relationships? It is a conundrum, really. But we can learn these things, and then attract those who like us for who we are. I wish I had learnt about vulnerability and solitude long ago.

When my relationships failed, I was filled with doubt and guilt for the longest time. It is natural to have these emotions. But a relationship is not really dependent only on you. You cannot pull on a relationship alone, ever. I always tried to fix them. Clearly, they were not meant to be. These were not even fulfilling relationships, but I had attached my self-worth to the outcome. It was really an unconscious decision to judge myself on the success of my relationships. Even others might do it, but why does it matter so much? Wouldn't it be better to fail at something which is not good for you? Learn and grow from it. Find the one that actually helps you, makes you happier and makes you feel fulfilled.

Why do we cling to such unhealthy relationships as if our lives depended on the outcome? For me, I was always told, that you have to make it work. But if all my energy is going in to making it work, it will make me an empty shell. Is it really worth it? "It will be easier," said my heart. "Fuck it," said my mind. Trust me, when you get out of it, the world will not end. One very wise woman told me, that when you are growing and someone leaves you, that person didn't deserve the best of you, which was yet to come.

We have come into this world alone, yet we are constantly told we are not good enough alone. Well, I say you prove them wrong and become more than enough alone. If you pause for some time and obsess over your own self as much as you have obsessed over these relationships, you can do wonders. It is great if you find someone who makes you happy. 'Happy' is the keyword here. It should not be imperative, time-bound or rushed.

P.S. Do you feel unworthy, unloved and miserable when not in a relationship? Well, if you cannot love yourself, who else can? Ponder over this.

Affirmation: I love myself irrespective of my relationship status and the success of my relationships.

DO ONE THING EVERY DAY THAT SCARES YOU – ELEANOR ROOSEVELT

Self-Worth and Failures

(Outcome of our projects)

The need to succeed has been drilled into us since we were little babies. How many times have your family or mentors told you to go have fun, and not worry if you fail? Did they really mean it, or was it a veiled pseudo technique of putting more pressure on you? Since childhood, I felt really pressured in all departments. I didn't have enough friends. Obviously, I have always been weird, or let's say unique, in my own way. I always see right through people since I was a child, and nothing pissed off people more than that. I felt like the young Sheldon a bit. I was too thin to look any good. My nickname was Hangar for God's sake. When I grew up, I had to be successful and find a suitable person to be with. And I was successful in finding them, suitable they were not.

Like my father said jokingly, you find a new monkey every year (he is funny, my father, gotta give it to him). Also, I had to motivate myself by educating myself with this notion, climb this hill and you will find the rainbow. Nothing like that happened. In pursuit of all these projects, I dared not fail, even if I was not learning anything of real importance. So I did it by the way. Skip hop jump from one success to another with God's grace, of course. I had perfect grades, looked perfect, had a ton of friends, a good job, a good on-paper husband, designer clothes and a room full of shoes, but I knew Zilch.

Because self-worth has nothing to do with these things. We just build a safety net with our so-called successes in this world to boost our self-esteem. It is not the same. Maybe having a great job might give a boost to your self-esteem at any given point, but one comment from your mean boss and you will be in shambles. All that joy will evaporate. Why does that happen? Your self-worth should not come from a job or how good you are at it, as you were made to believe. It should come from you trusting yourself and having unwavering faith in your worth as a human being, irrespective of what you have and how you have succeeded. It is valuing yourself and knowing yourself completely.

And does success teach you that? My friend, you will be surprised, but success is mostly outward. Only failure can teach you to look inside. Only the pain that comes with failure can unlock the treasure within. Failure is your best friend—it shows you all that needs patching up. Dare to fail! Hold failure's hand, take a stroll and have a conversation when it comes. Take it out for a coffee. After all, one heartbreak can teach you more than all your good relationships put together.

It also makes you a much better person. I was kind of an asshole with too many shoes before I failed at stuff generally in life. "Also, what doesn't kill you makes you stronger," said Friedrich Nietzsche. It also liberates you from all the pressure to be successful. You can basically try new stuff, as you yourself are not sure of their success. And sometimes your best work is after you have failed a lot, as you stop giving any effs. I am making it sound so tempting. See, I am not asking you to fail on purpose, but if you do, do try to learn the most out of it and remember it can be good also. I want you to try things despite the fear and possibility of failure. Try it, you won't regret it. What's the worst that can happen?

P.S. This chapter is owed to the failure of all social media platforms at 2 am, July 4th, 2019. As I had nothing else to do, I wrote this chapter. Failure can lead to good things, even new things you have never imagined. Failure makes you a badass in the real sense, and you go after things you never would otherwise. It is true.

Affirmation: I now know how to build on my failures and turn them into success.

I CAN ACCEPT FAILURE, BUT I CAN'T ACCEPT NOT TRYING – MICHAEL JORDAN

The Domino Effect

Sometimes in your life, you face a time of grave injustice (that is what we call it when we are in the victim mentality). A learned person might call it a time of great learning and growth.

In such a phase, whatever you touch turns to sand and flows out of your hand. And me, I had major control issues, so I was flabbergasted. I did what anyone would do. I asked, "Why? Why? Why Me? What have I done?" But it was like watching falling dominoes. Have you seen it? It exactly describes what was happening in my life. I tried hard, but failures came one after another. It affected my emotional health, then my physical health, my career and also all the weak links in my life. This light shone, shone upon the chinks in my armour. I was exhausted and soul-tired. It is a thing, let me tell you that. The domino effect crushes your soul and shakes you till you have realisations of epic proportions. This is called the 'Dark Night of the Soul' by some. If you manage to stay moderately successful, you will not be affected. We only seek help when we are crushed or pushed into a corner and are extremely desperate. And desperate I was.

But then, when nothing seems to be working, the indomitable human spirit finds a way. In that dark place, you will find valuable things. You try doing something, anything you can. I found out I was good at researching and learning. So I learnt. I learnt Reiki, astrology, Theta, Merlin and finally Kriya yoga. I read innumerable books on karma and ancestral karma. I researched the shit out of my dark phase, and I learnt the deep spiritual reasons of my phase, and I found out why. Then I gladly learnt my lessons, well, mostly. There were days I lay on the floor and kicked my legs in the air. I have always been a good student. I found my gifts of creativity and much more. Like J K Rowling said, failure took away all the unnecessary things and pushed her to write. Sometimes failure reveals the expendables for you and deflects you in the right direction. After all, when you hit rock bottom, you can go up the way you like.

But when I look back at it, no amount of success could have made me so strong and grounded. It is not fun, this phase. You might not even have such a dark phase in your life, but do not undervalue yourself just because you fail at something. Just learn from it. **"Everything that happens is for you, not to you" — Tony Robbins.** We are here to grow and nothing else.

P.S. I would like to say I am moderately successful right now. The day I become super successful, I will treat all my friends who were kind enough to me during this phase and never left my side. I will tell them one by one so I can better manage it. Hush hush, beaming smile. This chapter is dedicated to all of them who supported me and never let go of their confidence in me, even when I did.

Affirmation: I will pass through all tough phases of my life with flying colours and use these phases to learn and grow as a person.

PATIENCE CAN BE BITTER BUT HER FRUIT IS ALWAYS SWEET – HABEEB AKANDE

The Green-Eyed Monster

Life always looks easier on other people somehow, and social media does not help. Look at anyone's life online—they are travelling, eating the best food, wearing their best clothes and posting their best pics. No one is posting the truth. Whenever I write the truth online sans humour, it is not appreciated. E.g., if I write that "the last seven years were pretty meh, and brought me anxiety for long periods, and I ate a lot during those periods to make up for it," do you think people will read about it? We can try, of course, but it won't fly. I think it's slightly unfair on the readers if I share my best moments and not my worst. People who read me should appreciate both, but that is just me, I guess.

So when you are emotionally low and you think about scrolling through your social media pages… worst idea! Everyone is super happy, or at least pretending to be, and it will turn you into a green-eyed monster. We all have emotions like anger, greed, jealousy, ego and hurt. Essentially, we all have ten heads of emotions, and killing the Raavan actually signifies our victory over these.

Tough luck! Now you will say you are a fulfilled person and not jealous of anyone. Well, do you even believe yourself? It takes a fair share of work to overcome and understand that everything is transient. Without doing that, it is difficult for you to have no emotion of jealousy unless you were born a saint. Maybe you haven't paid attention to it, but it is there, as it is a legitimate human emotion.

Consciously or unconsciously, we are all jealous human beings. We want what others have. We want that love, that dress, that hot boyfriend, that hot body, that house which belongs to someone else. We aren't getting it as it is their good karma or hard work, but we like to torture ourselves.

Why do we have such cravings, and how can we get rid of them? First of all, ask that person how they have achieved it. Usually, a lot of blood, sweat and tears are involved in achieving anything. Secondly, maybe they are going through a good phase. Life is a roller coaster; we are all travelling in the same direction, and you will pass the same point after some time. Thirdly, detach your self-worth from materialistic things, from things that you own. These things only give you a temporary feeling of increased self-worth. The feeling only lasts a couple of days, even if you get that thing. E.g., Even if you get that cute boyfriend, but he won't text you back, or is controlling, or just keeps looking at himself, will you be happy? In two days, you will run for your life. We don't actually know yet the sacrifices that will have to be made to have him in your life.

If God comes and tells you that you can have those washboard abs, but you cannot eat any of your favourite things, and you need to work out 4 hours every day, Are you ready to do it? Maybe you will settle somewhere in between, like having a cute body and also having your favourite foods. Do we really need what the other person has? Very unlikely. What makes the other person happy might not make you happy. And if you are sure, get inspired, and not jealous. It's good to get inspired for the right reasons. Do not measure yourself against anyone. Measure yourself against yourself, and that too, not often. Only once in a while.

P.S. Sharing some of the things I wanted to post online but didn't. My worst moments of the year:

1. This month, I overslept almost every day and then felt guilty about it. #morningssuck — February.
2. I was walking on the road, and I fell on all fours, and a lot of people saw that. I practically rolled like a drum on the inclined road. I twisted my left ankle, and had to use crutches and also cried buckets. Feeling extra sad — May.
3. I was walking my dog, and we were attacked. I was bitten on my bum by a stray dog, and I had to take injections. My bum is scarred for life, but not my relationship with stray dogs. Because that dog kind of came and apologised later on — June.

Affirmation: My self-worth is independent of the achievements of other people.

KINDNESS IS ALWAYS FASHIONABLE, AND ALWAYS WELCOME – AMELIA BARR

Self-Worth and the Opposite Sex Loving You

To be very honest, when I started this book, I thought the last chapter would be the chapter about how I found the perfect person for me. This chapter is exactly the opposite of that. Clearly, I haven't found The One, but I did realise how much my emotional happiness depended on it. I completed this book last year, but it felt incomplete. I wrote this chapter today, on the 27th of March, 2023, to complete this book.

This is by far the most difficult thing I have written because owning up to your bullshit is not easy. Before I wrote this book, I wasn't happy because my self-worth was totally attached to a member of the opposite sex loving me. I swear it was so conditionally inherent in my personality, so deep down that I wasn't aware of it myself. At this point, I love myself, kids love me, my cousins love me, and aunties love me (I am lying, they don't love anyone). Even the plants and flowers have started loving me. Animals are crazy in love with me now. Still waiting for that one man to love you to get insanely happy seems a bit unnecessary. It's only the icing on the cake if and when it happens. Be insanely happy without the need for The One.

I am not against love. I love love. But it is a dangerous thing to attach your self-worth to one member of the other sex loving you. We are so much more than that. Yes, I have met people whose self-worth is attached to getting married, having children and running a home. It is all good if that is what makes you happy. But what if you want to become a biker or a mountaineer? Then you must detach yourself from this regular societal plan with timelines. It is imprinted in our DNA, due to the societal belief system, that we were born for this. We were not, and we don't need a member of the opposite sex to be happy. It's your choice, and if you wish to have a dozen children, go for it, but give the other person the right to make that choice. Give yourself the right to make the choice.

I just want to be left alone while I decide what makes me happy. Don't you?

Affirmation: My self-worth is independent of the validation of the opposite sex in any way.

IN ORDER TO FLY, YOU MUST FIRST LET GO OF EVERYTHING THAT WEIGHS YOU DOWN – UNKNOWN

About the Author

Priyannsha is a marketer, entrepreneur and retail professional with over 12 years of experience in retail and marketing. She has launched many international brands in India and has co-founded a marketing BTl firm called IKIGAI in Bangalore, launching many boutique brands. She is a NIFT graduate and has a Marketing degree from U C Berkeley, San Francisco. In her professional life, she currently works as a marketer in a Global Consulting firm.

Outside of professional life, she is a ***Kriya*** Yogi and a Merlin Practitioner. She is a spiritual coach and a Karmic healer. She loves to write about the unknown and unusual that cannot be seen with the naked eye. She went into deep consciousness to do all the self-work over many years and thus was able to write her first book, called ***Never Been Single*** (*A Journey of Self-Worth*). This book will bring that consciousness to the reader, and they will benefit from the author's journey. The author considers the book not only her wish but her moral obligation to share what she has realised. She is also editing her second book, currently called *A Gift of Story*, which will help parents and children to build a solid spiritual base. While her first book acts like a relationship coach, the second book, she believes, would act like a Life Coach.

She runs a Spiritual community called ***Pinkflamingo***, aimed at making people happier and kinder. She is also a blogger (www.pinkflamingo.life) and writes on spiritual topics like karma, familial relationships, patriarchy, implicit beauty standards, etc. Many of her articles have been published in online spiritual journals and lifestyle magazines, and were very well appreciated by the readers. She has a YouTube channel with the series ***For the Love of Navagraha*** (which explains the spiritual implications of astrology in our lives) and books that changed her life. She enjoys long walks and exploring new cafes, and loves spending time with animals and nature.

You can find her online, via her Instagram:
@pinkflamingoliv or her Facebook community at
Pinkflamingolife.